D1470121

LAW ENFORCEMENT

Zachary A. Kelly

The Rourke Corporation, Inc.
Vero Beach, Florida 32964

PHOTO CREDITS:
Tony Gray: cover, pages 12, 22, 32, 34, 37; © U.S. Dept. of Justice: pages 4, 16, 20, 36; Danny Bachelor: pages 6, 7, 9, 24, 26, 27, 28, 29, 39; East Coast Studios: pages 14, 42, 44; © Earl Young/Archive Photos: page 19

PRODUCED BY: East Coast Studios, Merritt Island, Florida

EDITORIAL SERVICES:
Penworthy Learning Systems

Library of Congress Cataloging-in-Publication Data

Kelly, Zachary A., 1970-
    Law enforcement / by Zachary Kelly.
        p. cm. — (Law and order)
    Includes index.
    Summary: Describes the work and importance of different kinds of law enforcement officers, discussing local and state officers, federal officers and organizations, and the cooperation of private citizens.
    ISBN 0-86593-574-2
    1. Law enforcement Juvenile literature. 2. Police Juvenile literature. [1. Police.
2. Law enforcement.] I. Title. II. Series.
HV7922.K45   1999
363.2—dc21   99-28689
                                                                       CIP

Printed in the USA

TABLE OF CONTENTS

Symbol of the U.S. Secret Service branch of law enforcement.

CHAPTER ONE

TO PROTECT AND TO SERVE

Law enforcement officers do a lot more every day than drive police cars and investigate crimes. They work to make our cities and states as safe as possible. The police have the goal to protect and to serve the people in their area. To protect people, police enforce laws, like a teacher enforces the rules of his or her classroom. They also keep people from violating the rights of others. Police protect us by investigating crimes, arresting suspects, and controlling large crowds. The police also serve people by helping them, even when no crime is involved.

Police assist people of all ages.

They search for missing children, help with traffic accidents, and hold activities, like basketball games. The men and women who work as law enforcement officers make a promise to protect and serve the people in their area—including you and your family.

Protecting people from crime and danger is a big job. **Federal officers** work all over the United States to capture suspects who have broken federal laws.

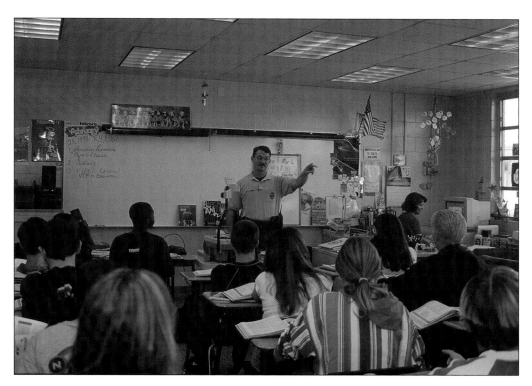

Many police officers go into schools to tell kids the officers' role in the community.

Federal laws are those laws that apply all over the country. State, county, and city officers protect people in their own areas. All police officers have several main jobs. When someone reports a crime, an officer goes to the scene to investigate the crime and get **evidence**. Once the police have a suspect, they **arrest** and keep the suspect until it's time to go to court. Police also keep watch to prevent crimes before they happen.

Law & Order Facts

The U.S. law enforcement community employed an average of 2.4 full-time officers for every 1,000 inhabitants as of Oct. 31, 1995.

Police are called to auto accident scenes to determine who might be at fault.

Sometimes keeping people safe means helping them when no one has done anything wrong. Police do that daily by giving directions to tourists or directing traffic at an accident scene or when a stoplight is not working. When a major storm or flood hits an area, police rescue people and set up shelters. They often sponsor programs to tell neighborhood people how to stay safe. Preventing crime is an important part of police work—just as important as dealing with crime after it happens.

CHAPTER TWO

LOCAL AND STATE OFFICERS

Each state has police at three levels: the state police, the county police, and the city police. Police at each level have different jobs. State police officers protect and serve the whole state. You have probably seen a police car patrolling a state highway near you. These officers enforce not only state traffic but also state hunting laws and laws concerning alcohol and drugs.

Several cities now have police on bikes patrol their busy, car-clogged streets.

A county police force covers a whole county. They take the place of municipal police in areas where towns are small and far apart. Usually, though, county police work outside cities and large towns. They help city police when needed and serve the many people who live outside the city limits. They enforce county laws and help investigate crimes in the county. County police head investigations when one person is a suspect in more than one part of the county. In this way, the city and county officers work together to solve crimes. If someone commits a crime in one county and then drives to another county, or commits crimes all over the state, the state police would call on county and city officers to help capture such a suspect.

An important service of state police results from their communication network. That network lets all officers in a state talk with each other. The network is handy for calling in county and city officers to help in emergencies.

The police force many of us know best is the **municipal** (city) police force. These police do the same kinds of jobs as state and county police. They enforce city laws, investigate crimes, and serve people; but they do it face to face. Some of the most important officers in the city police force are *patrol officers*. These officers work very hard to make our cities safe, but they are only one part of the city force. Another part of the city police force is the *criminal investigation division*. Here the detectives put evidence together to solve a crime.

This part of the police force also runs the crime lab, where officers work with **physical evidence**. The *traffic division* of the police force monitors traffic and provides licenses and tags for cars. Officers in the *community service division* provide health education and school programs and work on other community affairs.

All states in the U.S. have state police agencies known as state troopers or the state patrol.

CHAPTER THREE

FEDERAL OFFICERS AND ORGANIZATIONS

City, county, and state police do most of the law enforcement in our country. Sometimes, though, someone commits crimes in more than one state or breaks a law of the federal criminal code. The federal code applies to the whole country. When someone breaks one of these laws, federal officers take the case.

There are about 50 federal law enforcement agencies in the U.S. The officers in these agencies work much like local police, but federal police have specific jobs. Federal law enforcement agencies include the U.S. Marshals, the Federal Bureau of Investigation (FBI), and the Immigration and Naturalization Service (INS).

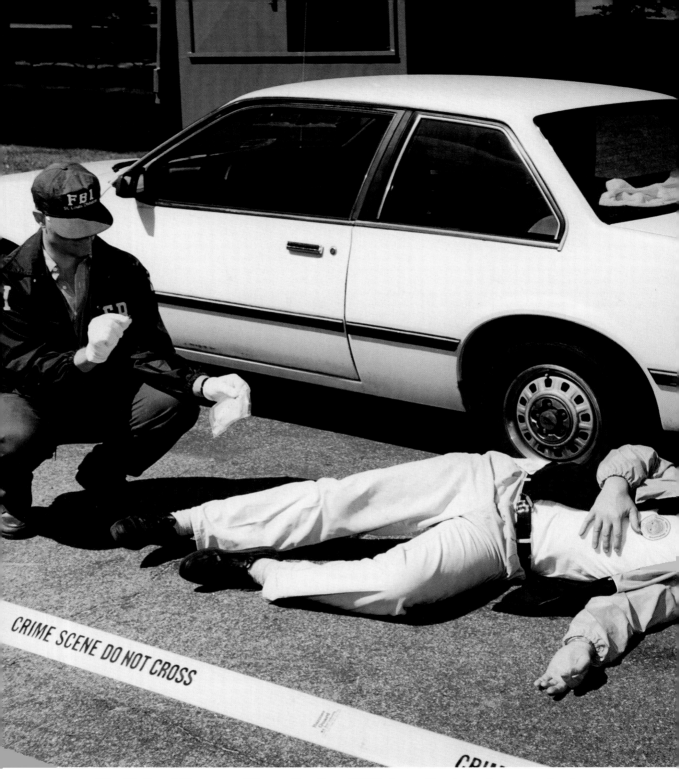

The Federal Bureau of Investigation (FBI) investigates crimes against the federal government.

The U.S. Marshals are the oldest police force in our country. The President appoints all 94 marshals to work with the federal courts. The marshals and their 1,500 deputies provide security for federal courthouses around the country. They also protect federal judges and lawyers if someone has threatened them. The marshals keep federal prisoners in custody and find suspects who are hiding. They also run the witness protection program, which protects people who might be in danger because they gave evidence against a criminal in court. A marshal cannot investigate a crime, though.

In 1908, Theodore Roosevelt created the **FBI**. The law establishing the agency stated that the FBI could investigate federal crimes and enforce federal laws. It is now the largest federal police force in the nation, with over 8,000 employees. FBI agents investigate federal crimes, apprehend suspects, and watch constantly to prevent crimes before they happen.

These officers keep huge amounts of information to help them catch criminals, including fingerprints, pictures, papers, and officers' reports. The FBI does not patrol streets like city police, but they work in every city to prevent federal crimes and protect the public from criminals.

You may not know the INS by name, but you may have heard of one of its departments, the Border Patrol. The Border Patrol guards U.S. borders against drug smugglers and illegal immigrants. They have stations in Florida, Texas, California, and other states. Besides watching the borders, these officers look for people who came to the U.S. illegally and help send them home.

The U.S. Border Patrol constantly patrols our borders—24 hours a day, seven days a week.

The INS also helps legal immigrants get the papers needed to get jobs and become U.S. citizens. Local police and federal agents fight crime in different ways. Working together, they protect all of us.

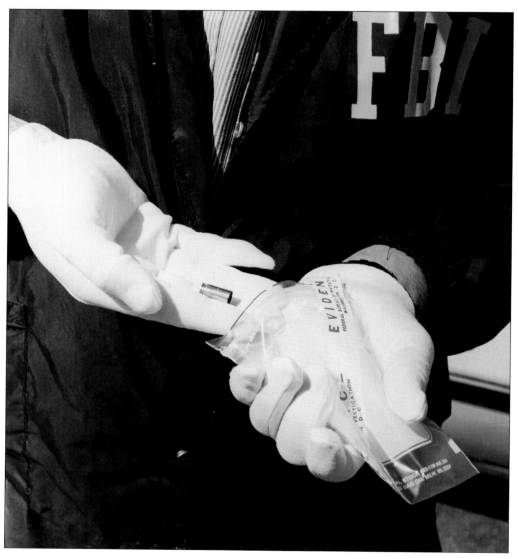

An investigator collects and stores a piece of evidence.

CHAPTER FOUR

JURISDICTION

Jurisdiction is a big word with a simple meaning. A police officer's **jurisdiction** is the area in which he or she works. It may be an area, like the northeast section of a city, or it may be an area of law. For example, a U.S. marshal can make arrests; but investigating is not in a marshal's jurisdiction. When a crime covers more than one area, officers with different jurisdictions work together to solve the crime. Sometimes it is clear who has jurisdiction in a case—but not always.

College students can report crimes directly to the police force on campus.

If someone reports a crime in a city, the municipal police respond—the city is their jurisdiction. If a crime occurs in a state park, the park police deal with it. If a suspect crosses a county line, the police in both counties work together to make an arrest. Most officers try to stay out of other officers' jurisdictions and assist only when needed. This keeps law enforcement officers from interfering with each other at a crime scene. Sometimes, though, the jurisdiction is unclear. Imagine that someone steals a car on a college campus in the middle of a big city. Most colleges have a police force to address crimes on campus, but stealing a car is a federal crime. Someone on the campus force probably would call the city police and perhaps the state police, too. Since car theft is a federal offense, local agents likely would call in federal officers. Whenever a crime crosses jurisdictions, agencies work together to solve it.

Jurisdiction within areas of law affects how officers work. In most municipal forces, separate departments handle different areas of the law. Once patrol officers respond to a case, for example, they may turn it over to another department, such as the investigation department. From there, the detectives take over and the patrol officers assist. The case is not in the patrol officers' jurisdiction anymore. State police forces use the same idea. They deal with state crimes and stay out of municipal and county police business as much as possible. Federal police also work within their jurisdiction. Jurisdiction allows police to do their jobs and to work together with other forces to protect and serve the public.

Police have access to many types of vehicles—including aircraft—to help them in their work.

CHAPTER FIVE

WORKING TOGETHER

Law enforcement officers often work together to fight crime. When different groups work together, each group works within its jurisdiction. The groups always must be in touch to avoid overlapping their work and wasting time. Police from different jurisdictions share several things when they work together. They share information, resources, and evidence. Every group of police has knowledge about its jurisdiction. Patrol officers in the municipal police force know their area of city and know much about many of the people who live there.

Law enforcement officers share information and receive updates on crimes before they start work each day.

This knowledge is sometimes the key to solving a case. State troopers might be very familiar with a certain stretch of highway where drivers often speed. The FBI has a huge amount of information about government workers, previous crimes, and convicted criminals. When different groups of officers work together, they often share case information. Sharing knowledge is a powerful way to fight crime.

The most important part of a shared operation is evidence. When several groups work on a case, each group usually looks for different kinds of evidence. Take a convenience store robbery, for example. The patrol officers would look for witnesses.

The investigation team would look for physical evidence at the store. If a state agency is involved, they may look for similar crimes in the state. Federal officers might join the case and find information about suspects. Police forces collect these facts, called *data*, and store them in a computer.

The computer program they use is called a *database*. A database puts data in order so that it is easy to find when needed. Officers can search a database quickly and get facts related to a case. Communication between them keeps them from looking at the same data twice and brings in evidence one group might not have on its own. Police often solve crimes by sharing data from their databases.

Local law enforcement officers patrol the streets on motorcycles and bikes and in cars.

In many cities dogs assist police in capturing suspects, keeping officers from harm.

Law enforcement officers also work with local communities in the fight against crime. Most police departments have organizations that bring officers and citizens together. Examples include the Fraternal Order of Police (FOP), Police Benevolent Association (PBA), and Police Athletic League (PAL). These organizations give police a way to serve the public above and beyond law enforcement. They also give police a chance to know how the citizens support their work. Another way police work with their communities is through education. Local, state, and federal departments have booklets for citizens interested in what police do. Police often go to public schools and college campuses to talk with students about safety, drug use, or crimes that may affect them.

CHAPTER SIX

ENFORCING LAWS

Laws are enforced when someone suffers consequences for not obeying them. To enforce classroom rules, a teacher may correct a student who breaks them. This correction makes students see that rules are important. It also gives them a good reason to follow the rules. If students obey the rules, their teacher does not have to correct them. Police officers do the same thing to get people to obey laws. When someone breaks laws, police enforce those laws with tickets, fines, or arrests.

Police officers may take anyone into custody for questioning if they suspect a crime has been committed.

Patrol officers do most of the law enforcement. Most police look at the circumstances as they enforce the law. If someone raced down the highway at 100 miles an hour, an officer may stop the car to give the driver a ticket for speeding. If the driver were taking an injured person to a hospital, though, the officer might help the driver, rather than give him or her a ticket. This condition is called police discretion. Police also have the right to stop a driver who looks suspicious. If an officer suspects that someone is committing or about to commit a crime, the officer can stop the person to search and/or ask questions.

If the officer believes a person acts suspicious, the officer has a good reason to stop the person. Another name for good reason is *probable cause*. An officer has probable cause to stop a suspect.

Police do not want to arrest innocent people. They also do not want criminals to get away. To avoid mistakes, police *investigate* a situation before they arrest anyone.

Law & Order Facts

"It is of the highest importance in the art of detection to be able to recognize out of a number of facts which are incidental and which are vital. . .".
Sir Arthur Conan Doyle (1859-1930)

A simple investigation happens each time police pull a car over. The police witnessed the offense, the first step of an investigation. Then they call the state traffic department to get information about the driver. If the driver happens to be a suspect in a crime, the officer will often arrest him or her right there. If not, the officer may issue a ticket or release the driver. When a more complicated crime happens and the police do not know who did it, they investigate thoroughly. Some investigations take months or years of painstaking effort on the part of police.

A local police officer writes a ticket for a parking violation.

CHAPTER SEVEN

SOLVING CRIMES

Once someone has committed a crime, law enforcement officers want to find out who did it. Their job is to solve the crime. When a court convicts a suspect, police consider the case solved. Police investigate all the information they can find about a crime, including when and where the crime happened, how it was done, and why. Once officers answer all of these questions, they usually know who committed the crime. Some cases are easy, as when an officer or other **eyewitness** sees the crime, or when the criminal confesses. Police look to witnesses and evidence when solving a crime.

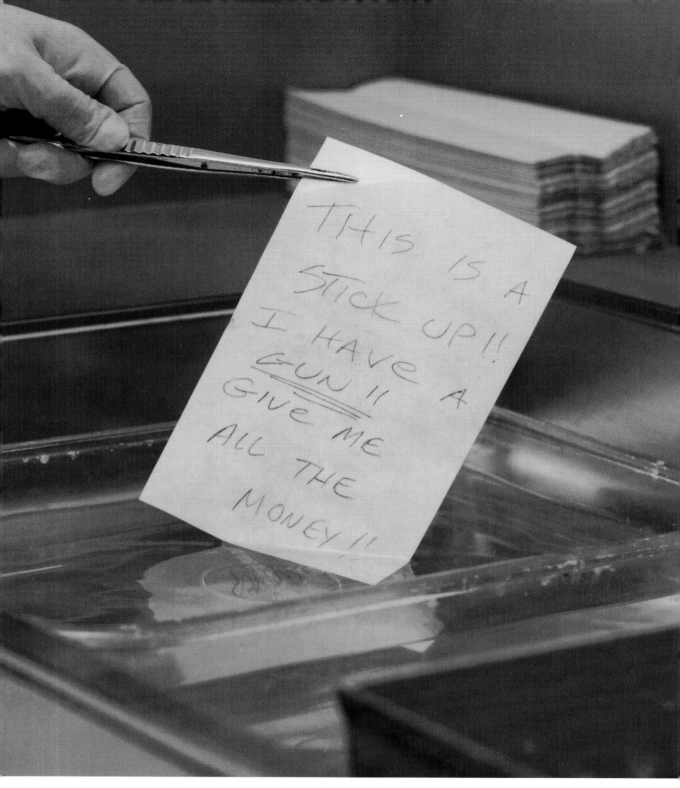

A simple handwritten note can be evidence.

A **witness** is someone who can give the police information about the crime or suspect. An eyewitness is someone who saw the crime being committed. Police use eyewitnesses to identify suspects' faces or voices and to give details about the events. Sometimes police make a **lineup**. A lineup is a line of people formed for an eyewitness to review. Police want to see if the witness can point out the suspect from the others in the lineup.

Law enforcement officers take detailed notes to complete reports about complaints or crimes.

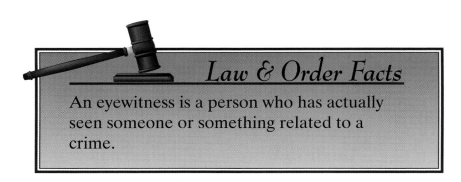

Police choose all kinds of people for the line-up, including other officers. If the witness identifies the suspect as the lineup walks by, then police are more certain they have arrested the right individual. In a trial, police will sometimes use **expert witnesses** to provide information about details related to crimes, such as a jeweler to identify a diamond. Other valuable information from witnesses includes seeing the suspect in the area at the time of the crime, talking to the suspect about the crime, or knowing the suspect personally.

Another key to solving a crime is evidence. Police use two kinds of evidence to solve cases. These are *circumstantial* evidence and *physical* evidence. Circumstantial evidence is a fact that points to an individual but is not enough to convict the person.

Local police and fire department assist in a traffic accident.

Examples of circumstantial evidence include buying a gun before a crime, being in the area during a crime, matching a witness's description, and having a motive for committing a crime. Such evidence may help the police, but it is not enough on its own to convict a suspect. Physical evidence is usually required to convict a person. Physical evidence includes any object that identifies a suspect, such as hair, clothing, fingerprints, and bullets at the crime scene. Police use all three—physical evidence, circumstantial evidence, and statements—to solve crimes.

CHAPTER EIGHT

WHAT CAN YOU DO?

If you are interested in learning more about laws and law enforcement, you can take several steps. Groups such as the Boy Scouts, Girl Scouts, and the Boys and Girls Clubs of America have activities and programs related to law enforcement. Schools, churches, and civic clubs often have activities that can bring you closer to law enforcement. For example, many schools participate in the D.A.R.E program. The letters stand for Drug Abuse Resistance Education. D.A.R.E. began in 1983, the work of the Los Angeles Police Department (LAPD) and the Los Angeles Unified School District.

Law enforcement officers work with the public to promote the D.A.R.E. program.

Since then, D.A.R.E. programs have been started in many schools around the country. In each program, the school and a local police department or county sheriff's office together provide activities for young people. Most D.A.R.E. programs to try alert young people to the dangers of illegal drugs or gangs. Participants in the program are taught how to respond if someone tries to sell or give them illegal drugs or a gang tries to attack or recruit them.

Many local police departments have special programs for young people. Some states have a law enforcement explorer program. If you join the explorers, you can visit police training schools, see officers do their daily work, learn about law enforcement techniques, and even help officers do such things as direct traffic at a big event. Explorers wear special uniforms and meet regularly, usually at a school or police department. Another group, Community Oriented Policing (COP), often sponsors activities and programs for young people.

Your community likely has groups that help young people learn about law and order. You can begin by asking your family, teachers, or the police in your area to help you get involved.

Many neighborhoods help police prevent crimes by creating neighborhood watch programs. This sign tells criminals that neighbors are watching for them.

GLOSSARY

arrest (uh REST) — seize and hold a person by authority of law

convict (KUN VIKT) — find or prove someone guilty of a crime, also (KAHN VIKT) a person found guilty of an offense or crime

circumstantial evidence (SER kuhm STAN shul EV eh dens) — indirect evidence that may help a judge or jury decide a case

evidence (EV eh dens) — statements by witnesses and objects (physical evidence) that identify a suspect

expert witness (EK spert WIT nis) — person called as a witness because of his or her great knowledge of a certain subject in a case

eyewitness (I WIT nis) — witness who saw the events of a given court case

FBI (FBI) — Federal Bureau of Investigation

federal officers (FED er ul AW fi serz) — officers who enforce federal laws

jurisdiction (JOOR is DIK shuhn) — area in which an officer or court has authority or control

GLOSSARY

line-up (LIEN UP) — line of people formed for identifying a crime suspect

municipal police (myoo NIS uh pul puh LEES) — police force of a city, town, village, or township

physical evidence (FIZ i kul EV eh dens) — things presented to a court that may help decide a case

witness (WIT nis) — one called to testify before a court

FURTHER READING

- Brown, Lawrence. *The Supreme Court.* Washington, D.C.: Congressional Quarterly, 1981.
- Conklin, John E. *Criminology.* Allyn and Bacon: Needham Heights, Mass, 1995.
- De Sola, Ralph. *Crime Dictionary.* NY: Facts on File, 1988.
- Hill, Gerald and Hill, Kathleen. *Real Life Dictionary of the Law.* Los Angeles: General Publishing Group, 1995.
- Janosik, Robert ., ed. *Encyclopedia of the American Judicial System.* NY: Charles Scribner and Sons, 1987.
- Johnson, Loch K. *America's Secret Power (CIA).* Oxford: OUP, 1989.
- Kadish, Sanford H., ed. *Encyclopedia of Crime and Justice.* NY: The Free Press, 1983.
- McShane, M. and Williams, F., eds. *Encyclopedia of American Prisons.* NY: Garland, 1996.
- Morris, N. and Rothman, D., eds. *The Oxford History of the Prison.* Oxford: OUP, 1995.
- Regoli, Robert and Hewitt, John. *Criminal Justice.* Prentice-Hall: Englewood Cliffs, NJ, 1996.
- Renstrum, Peter G. *The American Law Dictionary.* Santa Barbara, CA: ABC-CLIO, 1991.
- Territo, Leonard, et al. *Crime & Justice in America.* West: St. Paul, MN, 1995.
- *The Constitution of the United States.* Available in many editions.
- *The Declaration of Independence.* Available in many editions.
- Voigt, Linda, et al. *Criminology and Justice.* McGraw-Hill: New York, 1994.

- http://entp.hud.gov/comcrime.html
  Crime Prevention
  Department of Justice
  PAVNET (Partnership Against Violence Network)
  Justice Information Center
- http://www.fightcrime.com/lcrime.htm
  Safety and Security Connection
  The Ultimate Guide to Safety and Security
  Resources on the Internet
- http://www.internets.com/spolice.htm
  Police Databases
- http://www.psrc.com/lkfederal.html
  Links to most Federal Agencies
- http://www.dare-america.com/
  Official Website of D.A.R.E.

INDEX